MILNER CRAFT SERIES

Bread Dough Creations

MILNER CRAFT SERIES

Bread Dough Creations

SUSAN ROACH

SALLY MILNER PUBLISHING

First published in 1993 by
Sally Milner Publishing Pty Ltd
558 Darling Street
Rozelle NSW 2039 Australia

Reprinted 1993

Design and illustrations by Anna Warren
Photography by Andrew Elton
Typeset in Australia by Asset Typesetting Pty Ltd
Printed in Australia by Impact Printing, Melbourne

National Library of Australia
Cataloguing-in-Publication data:

Roach, Susan (Susan Sheree).
  Bread dough creations
  ISBN 1 86351 102 4.

  1.Bread dough craft. 2. Handicraft. I. Title.
  (Series: Milner craft series).

745.5

Acknowledgements

Thank you to all those who helped me put this book together, in particular Sally Milner and her expert team and Andrew Elton for his beautiful photography. Furthermore I would like to thank Anna Warren for her fine illustrations.

I would also like to thank Timber Turn, Selleys and Matisse paints for their support.

A special thank you to my children Sarah, Kent and Emily for their unconditional love and finally to my husband David for his encouragement, support and love; without it, this would have still been a dream.

Susan Roach 1993

Contents

Introduction

The South American Indians were reportedly the first people to use bread dough to make artistic pieces of ornamentation centuries ago. They lived in Ecuador and, having little access to clay, they created their own recipes for bread dough.

During the second world war women made bread dough jewellery, as it was the only type of jewellery available during those hard times. The original recipes did not include glue and the jewellery had to be dusted and kept in a warm place at all times to prevent mould forming.

I have spent the past 10 years refining my own recipes and I now happily pass my knowledge of this craft to you, the reader, so you can create your own bread dough pieces.

Susan Roach

Material Stockists

Bread — white sliced bread, which can be obtained from your local milk bar, delicatessen or supermarket

Glues — I prefer to use Selleys Aquadhere and Selleys 5-minute Araldite. Glues can be obtained from your local hardware store

Paints — I prefer to use Matisse acrylic paints. Paints can be obtained from your local craft store, newsagent or art supplies shop

Varnish — use a semi-gloss water-based varnish, which can be obtained from your local hardware store

Palettes — available from your local craft or art supplies shop

Cutters — available from any cake decorating supplies shop

Glossy cardboard for templates — available from newsagents or art supplies shops

Wood accessories — I prefer to use products from Timber Turn Pty Ltd in Adelaide, South Australia

Stamens — available from any cake decorating supplies shop

Brooch backs — available from your local craft shop

Hair accessories — available from most chemist or department stores

Paint brushes — sponge and bristle brushes can be purchased from your local craft or art supplies shop

Bread Dough: The Beginning

Bread

Many people enquire how you could possibly make jewellery from bread. Not only can you, but it's inexpensive, the main ingredient being bread. All brands of sliced white bread are suitable.

Glues

Use a wood glue, such as Selleys Aquadhere, to knead the bread dough and to glue the pieces of dough onto the base. To find out about the proportion of crumbs to glue, see 'Preparing the dough'. Use a glue like Selleys Araldite to secure brooch backs. Mix glue carefully according to the instructions on the packet.

Paints

Acrylic paints such as Matisse achieve a variety of both traditional and exotic colours. The choice of colours is individual, but I suggest that you always mix white paint with the bread dough prior to adding other pigments.

Glaze finished products all over with a clear, water-based varnish for protection.

Palettes

You can use any type of palette, from an artist's palette to a very inexpensive ice-cream container lid. If there is any unused paint, or you need to take a short break, cover the palette with plastic wrap.

Cutters

Flower- and leaf-shaped cutters are illustrated below. For the purpose of identifying the cutters used in the book, each cutter has been numbered, and I refer to these numbers throughout the book. The cutters are easy to use, especially the ejector cutters. The cutters illustrated are exact sizes and are available at cake decorating supplies shops. When you wish to purchase your cutters, it is simply a matter of matching up the cutters with those in the book.

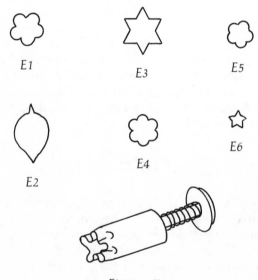

E1

E3

E5

E2

E4

E6

Ejector cutters

14

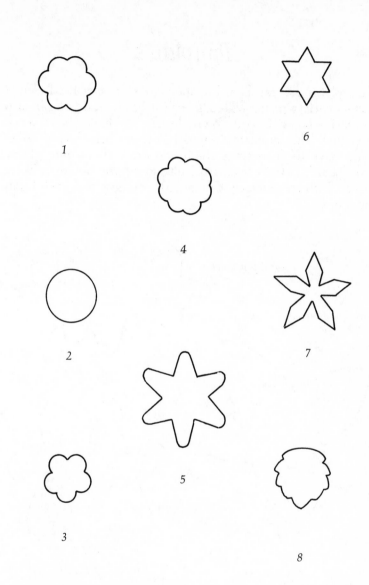

Aluminium cutters

Templates

Templates are cardboard shapes cut to a specific design. I use a variety of template shapes for bases, and you can also experiment with your own designs to make your work original. The template designs below are actual sizes, so all you have to do is trace them and draw them onto glossy cardboard. If the cardboard isn't glossy, the dough is likely to stick to the surface. Cut out the designs and keep them in a box.

Oval-leaf template

Four-leaf template

Round-leaf template

Name bar template

16

Jewellery box with assorted jewellery, cottage thimble and flower thimble

Hair ribbon holder

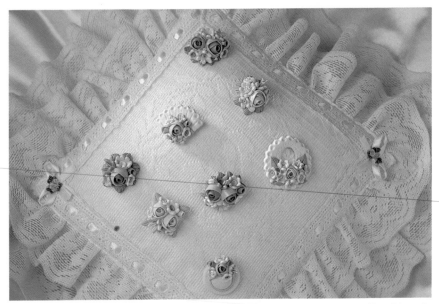

*An assortment of brooches: oval and round leaf brooches, fan brooch, oval scalloped brooch,
four-leaf brooch and hat brooch*

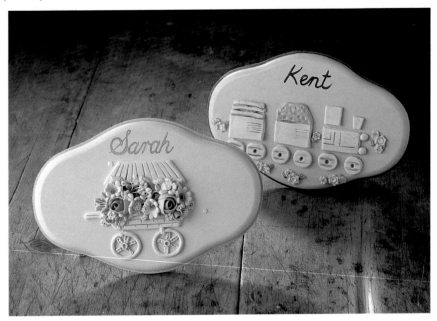

Children's plaques: flower cart name plaque and train name plaque

A selection of children's brooches: bird brooch, bunny brooch, butterfly brooch and some simple bar brooches

Hair accessories: tortoise shell combs, hair slides, auto hair clasp and head band

Photo frame and hand mirror

Tissue box holder

Wooden Accessories

You can use wood accessories such as tissue boxes, photo frames, door wedges and a variety of other items, all of which can be purchased from Timber Turn Pty Ltd. Prior to creating bread dough designs on wood, it will be necessary to prepare all wooden surfaces thoroughly, as explained in the 'Preparation of Wood' section.

Miscellaneous Items

- Scissors (small and pointed)
- Artists paint brushes
- 2 cm (¾") and 4 cm (1½") sponge brushes
- 40 cm x 30 cm (16" x 12") wooden board (smooth and laminated)
- Spatula (for mixing paints)
- Stitch unpicker (used in dressmaking)

(Break off the pointed end of stitch unpicker, leaving the ball end only. The rounded ball end is used for pressing the small dough balls into the centre of a flower, while the reverse end (handle) is used to shape the actual flowers.)

- Stamens (use for inside of flowers — various colours are available from cake decorating supplies shops. Cut stamens to fit into the middle of the moulded flower, i.e. approx. 1 cm (⅜").
- Small rolling pin
- Berri pins

(use the coloured ball ends for picking up and indenting)

- Scone cutters (straight and scalloped edges)
- Wire screen (any size)

(use to dry dough products naturally)

- Darning needles (use for making a leaf effect on bases)

Basic Techniques

Preparing the Dough

Use sliced white bread that is a few days' old as it is easier to crumb. Remove all the crusts from six slices of bread and crumb in a blender. Place the crumbs into an empty ice-cream container, add approximately 60 ml (¼ cup) of glue such as Aquadhere to the crumbs and mix with a wooden stick (ice block sticks are easy to stir with and you can throw them away after) until the glue has been dispersed evenly with the crumbs. The next step is messy but a very important part of the finished product.

Take a handful of dough and knead it with your hands. The dough will be sticky to start with, but will soften and become smoother as you knead. The dough is ready when it is very smooth and soft with no lumps. Always cover the dough with plastic wrap to prevent a dry crust forming and keep it supple. Use the dough within 10 days.

Colouring the Dough

Blend the soft dough with an acrylic white paint to give it a solid base consistency to which any other colour can be added later. I suggest around 2 tablespoons of white paint to a tennis ball sized amount of bread dough. Knead the paint into the dough to give it a very white appearance. The dough is now ready for other colours to be added.

Break away small sections of dough and knead in your chosen colour of acrylic paint. Start with a small 'dob' of coloured paint — you can always add more later. I prefer Matisse acrylic paints as they are economical and have a good range of colours.

18

Attaching the Shapes

When placing the bread dough flowers and shapes, etc. on the bases or objects, they are all glued into place using a glue such as Aquadhere.

Base Making

You can use the whitened dough to make bases. I colour the dough green for the jewellery bases as it contributes to the leafy appearance. I leave the dough white for the fan, oval scalloped and hat bases.

OVAL AND ROUND LEAF GREEN BASES

Roll out green dough to about 4 mm ($1/_6$") thick. Place the template onto the dough and press gently. Remove the template, and with sharp pointed scissors, cut the pattern out. Clean up the edges of the dough by using your fingers to smooth them. Use a darning needle to indent the vein pattern into the dough.

indent veins of leaf with a darning needle

OVAL SCALLOPED WHITE BASE

Roll out white dough to about 4 mm ($1/_6$") thick. Use a scone cutter about 50 mm (2") in diameter with a scalloped edge. After cutting out the shape, clean up the edges of the dough, and with a round cutter cut an off-centre hole about 16 mm ($2/_3$") in diameter. Pull the dough very gently with your fingers at opposite ends to form an oval shape. With a berri pin, indent a hollow shape in each scallop. Dry the dough on a screen.

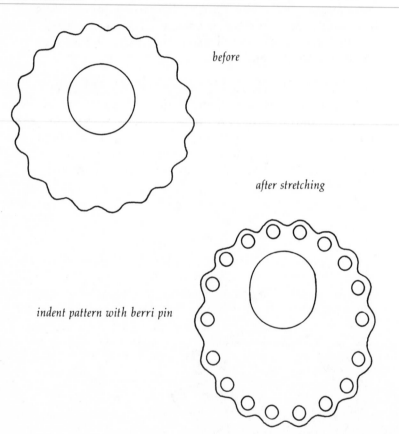

before

after stretching

indent pattern with berri pin

FOUR-LEAF GREEN BASE

Roll out green dough to about 4 mm ($^1/_6$″) thick. Place the four-leaf template onto the dough and press down gently. Cut the shape out with scissors and, using your fingers, smooth any rough edges. Use a darning needle to indent the veins of each large leaf. Dry the leaves on a screen.

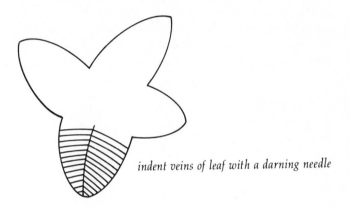

indent veins of leaf with a darning needle

NAME BAR BASE

Roll out white dough to about 4 mm ($^1/_6$″) thick. Place the bar template onto the dough and gently press down. Cut the design out with pointed scissors and, using your fingers, smooth any rough edges. This shape can be used as a name brooch or covered all over with flowers.

FAN BASE

Roll out white dough to about 4 mm ($^1/_6$") thick. Using the same scone cutter you used for the oval scalloped base, cut out a round shape and, using your fingers, smooth any rough edges of the dough. Using a ruler, cut a straight line into the dough across one way and then the other, leaving nine scalloped shapes at the top, and a 90° angled 'V' shape at the bottom. This gives you the fan shape. With a berri pin, indent into each scallop shape, leaving a hollow pattern. Finally, use a ruler to press into the dough, leaving a line separating each scallop edge. Dry the dough on a screen.

berri pin used to mould shape in scallop edges

use ruler to indent lines in fan

HAT BASE

Roll out white or any coloured dough to about 4 mm (¹/₆″) thick. Using a stone cutter or even a glass (port size) about 35 mm (1½″) in diameter, cut out the shape and tidy up the edge. Make a ball of dough about the size of an average marble, dip it in glue and place it in the middle of the circle shape. Gently press down so that it resembles a hat. Make a pattern with a darning needle in the dough on the flat part of the hat. Dry the dough on a screen.

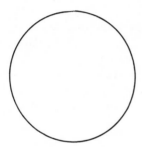

use a darning needle to pattern dough

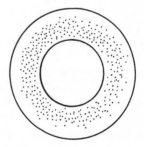

gently press dough to shape into top of hat shape

Rose making

The rose is one of the most frequently used flowers in bread dough jewellery. They require a lot of practice to make, but the results are beautiful.

Take a small piece of dough approximately the size of a marble and make a ball. Press one side of the ball flat. Lay the flat side across your thumb and roll inwards with the other hand to form the bud. Form a petal by following the same procedure, but do not roll inward. Instead roll the petal around the bud. Continue making petals, overlapping them progressively until four petals have been positioned around the bud.

After placing the petals around each other, squeeze the dough gently between your fingers to shape the base of the rose.

Cut off the excess dough with scissors. (See step-by-step photographs of this procedure in colour pages.)

A double bud is formed by adding one petal only to a single bud.

Preparation of Wood

Prepare all wood pieces carefully as they will affect the quality of the finished product. Wear a face mask and smock or apron when sanding wood pieces, and place the pieces on old newspaper. Fine grade sandpaper is usually appropriate. Remove all labels, hinges and hooks and keep them in a safe place. Fill wood imperfections with wood putty, and sand when dry. Use a sanding block to ensure that the wood is sanded evenly, and sand with the grain for the best results. After sanding, vacuum the wood or wipe it to remove dust particles.

Drying Procedures

Place all bread dough bases and finished ornaments onto an elevated wire screen. The elevated screen allows air to circulate under the bread dough, ensuring the dough dries evenly. Place the dough on screen in a warm area to facilitate the drying process. An alternative that will give you quick drying during summer or spring is to place the screen out in the sun.

Bread dough bases take two days to dry. Jewellery on bases takes two to three days to dry. Bread dough creations on wood take three to four days depending on the size of your creation.

Always work with moist dough and allow finished pieces to dry naturally on a screen. Finished products will shrink to about 75 per cent of their original size when completely dry.

Brush Care

Wash your brushes with soap and water and rinse them well. Preserve brushes by coating them in soap after use and then allowing to dry. Rinse brushes well before using them again. To avoid damaging your brushes, never leave the point of a brush sitting in water.

KEY

rose

double bud

single bud

1

2

3

4

5

6

7

8

E1

E2

E3

E4

E5

E6

26

Jewellery Collection

Oval Green Base Brooch

Prepare and dry an oval green base
Make two roses
Make one single bud
Make one double bud
Cut one number 1 shape
Cut one number 4 shape
Cut one number 5 shape
Cut three E1 shapes
Cut six E6 shapes

Place and glue the roses together across the centre of the brooch base, then gently glue the buds at either end of the roses. Using the handle end of a stitch unpicker, mould the number 1 shape, apply glue and push it gently into the sides of the roses. Repeat this with the number 5 shape and number 4 shape, and place each of the three E1 shapes into the open gaps. Cut three stamens about 10 mm (⅜") long, dip into glue and push into the centre of the number 5 shape. Make tiny balls of dough and glue one into the centre of each E1 shape, pressing them in with the ball end of a berri pin. Place the E6 shapes around the brooch.

Dry the brooch on a screen. When completely dry, glue

a brooch back onto the base, using a glue such as Selley's 5-minute Araldite. Leave for at least 15 minutes then glaze with a water-based varnish and leave to dry.

Round Green Base Brooch

Prepare and dry a round green base
Make one rose
Make one single bud
Cut one number 3 shape
Cut one number 4 shape
Cut one number 5 shape
Cut two E1 shapes

Place the rose and then the single bud onto the centre of the base. Using the rounded handle end of a stitch unpicker arrange the number 3, 4 and 5 shapes on the base to resemble a bunch of flowers. Using the round end of a berri pin, arrange the E1 shapes in the gaps. Cut three stamens about 10 mm (⅜") long, dip into glue and place into the centre of the number 5 shape. Place a tiny ball of dough into the centre of each remaining shape, press down and with the ball end of a stitch unpicker, indent a pattern into the dough.

Leave to dry on a screen. When dry, glue a brooch back onto the base with a glue such as a 5-minute Araldite. Glaze the brooch with a water-based varnish when dry.

Fan Brooch

Prepare and dry a fan brooch base
Make one rose
Make one double bud
Make one single bud
Cut three E2 shapes
Cut one number 3 shape
Cut one number 6 shape
Cut three E1 shapes

Place the three E2 shapes at the narrow end of the fan in a triangle shape. Arrange the rose at an angle close to the leaves, and the double and single buds at either side of the rose. Dip shapes number 3 and 6 in glue and use the handle end of a stitch unpicker to arrange them side by side on the base of the fan. Gently push the three E1 shapes into the gaps. Glue three 10 mm (⅜") long stamens into the centre of the number 6 shape.

Dry the brooch on a screen, then glue a brooch back to the base using 5-minute Araldite or similar. Glaze the brooch with a water-based varnish.

This is a sweet brooch, suitable also for children.

Hat Brooch

Prepare and dry a hat brooch base
Make one rose
Make one single bud
Make one double bud
Cut three E2 shapes
Cut one number 3 shape
Cut one number 6 shape
Cut three E1 shapes

Roll a small amount of coloured dough into a sausage shape. Apply a little glue along the sausage and wrap around the hat to make a ribbon effect. Push gently to flatten the dough slightly. Cut any excess dough away, but don't worry about the join as it will be covered with flowers. Place the rose over the join and arrange the buds on either side of it. Arrange the three E2 leaf shapes around the rose and buds. Mould the number 3 and number 6 shapes with the handle end of a stitch unpicker and place them next to each other on the hat near the roses. Put three 10 mm (⅜") stamens into the middle of the number 6 shape, and a tiny ball of dough into the centre of the number 3 shape, pressing into the ball with a berri pin. Arrange the E1 shapes into the gaps.

Dry the brooch on a screen and then glue a brooch back to the base, using a glue such as 5-minute Araldite. Glaze the brooch with a water-based varnish.

Four-Leaf Green Base Brooch

Prepare and dry a four-leaf green base
Make two roses
Make one single bud
Make one double bud
Cut three E1 shapes
Cut one number 1 shape
Cut one number 5 shape

Place the roses next to each other in the centre of the base and arrange the buds on each side of the roses. Using the handle end of a stitch unpicker mould shape number 1 (daisy) and place next to the roses. Place a tiny ball of dough into the centre of shape number 1, flatten slightly and pattern with the ball end of the stitch unpicker. On the opposite side to the daisy, place the number 5 shape and glue three 10 mm (⅜") stamens in its centre. Arrange the three E1 shapes in the gaps. Dry the brooch on a screen then glue a brooch back to the base with a glue such as 5-minute Araldite. Glaze the brooch with water-based varnish.

Oval Scalloped White Base Brooch

Prepare and dry an oval scalloped white base
Make one rose
Make two single buds
Cut two number 3 shapes
Cut three E1 shapes
Cut four E2 shapes
Cut two E3 shapes

Place the rose in the middle of the base just under the opening and arrange the four E2 shapes either side of it as in the drawing. Push the two number E3 shapes into the sides of the rose and glue two 10 mm (⅜") stamens into the centre of each. Arrange the remaining shapes in the gaps. When the brooch is completely dry, glue a small piece of lace on the back of the base to cover the hole. Glue a brooch back to the base with a glue such as 5-minute Araldite and glaze the brooch with water-based varnish.

Candle holders and napkin holders

Door hanger and door wedge

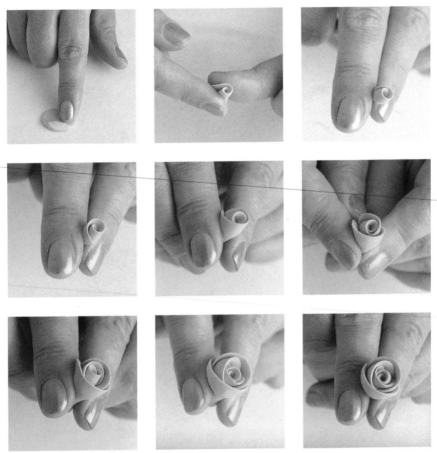

Making a bread dough rose

Top row, left: Press down one side of a small ball of bread dough

Top row, centre: Lay flat across thumb and roll inwards using index finger of other hand

Top row, right: Completed single bud

Middle row, left: To make a rose, commence with a single bud

Middle row, centre: Form a petal by flattening another ball of dough as described above. Roll the petal around the bud. (This is a double bud)

Middle row, right: Form another petal and, overlapping the first petal, roll around the bud

Bottom row, left: Overlap a third petal around the first two petals and bud

Bottom row, centre: Overlap a fourth petal and squeeze the base gently to shape the base of the rose

Bottom row, right: The completed rose

Bread dough can be applied to fabric to great effect as these examples show

Some of the many wooden objects that can be embellished with bread dough

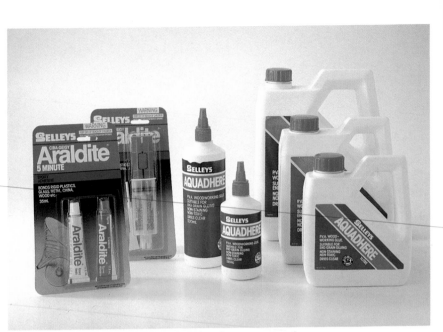

The type of glues used in bread dough embroidery

The type of paints used in bread dough embroidery

Hair Accessories

Tortoise Shell Hair Slide

Purchase a hair slide
Make one rose
Make two double buds
Make two single buds
Cut eight E4 shapes
Cut four E1 shapes

Etch the top surface of the hair slide with a cutting knife blade to enable the bread dough to adhere better. Roll out a sausage of green dough large enough to cover the top of the slide. You can pattern this base with leaf markings if you like. Glue the green dough to the top of the etched slide with a glue such as Aquadhere. Leave the slide to dry — this normally takes up to a day. When dry, place a rose in the centre of the base and glue the double buds either side of the rose and then the single buds on either side of the double bud. Place one E4 shape at each end of the slide and place remaining E4 shapes evenly around rose and buds. Push the E1 shapes into the gaps between the rose and buds (two on each side). Place a 10 mm (⅜") stamen into the centre of each E1 shape. When completely dry, glaze with water-based varnish.

I enjoy working with hair slides because they dry so quickly, and they are great presents to have on hand.

Tortoise Shell Auto Clasp

Purchase one auto clasp
Make one rose
Make two double buds
Make two single buds
Cut six E4 shapes
Cut four E1 shapes

Etch the top of the auto clasp with a cutting knife blade to enable the bread dough to adhere better. Roll enough green dough in the shape of a sausage to cover the top of the clasp. Glue the dough gently onto the clasp using a glue such as Aquadhere and make leaf patterns at each end with a darning needle if you wish. When dry (after about a day), place the rose in the centre of the clasp, glue a double bud on each side of the rose, then a single bud beside each double bud. Place E4 shapes along the clasp each side of the rose and buds. Fill in the gaps between the rose and buds with the E1 shapes and glue a 10 mm (⅜") stamen in the centre of each. When dry, glaze the clasp with water-based varnish.

Tortoise Shell Dressing Table Comb

Purchase one tortoise shell comb (straight or curved)
Make one rose
Make two double buds
Make two single buds
Cut six E4 shapes
Cut four E3 shapes

Etch the surface of the comb with a cutting knife blade to enable the bread dough to adhere easily. Make an 80 mm (3″) sausage shape of green bread dough, glue and press onto the top of the comb. Allow at least a day to dry, then place the rose in the middle of the base with a double bud on either side, followed by a single bud. Arrange the four E3 shapes, two on each side of the comb, between the rose and the double buds. Gently push in with the handle end of a stitch unpicker. Cut four stamens about 10 mm (⅜″) long and glue one in the centre of each E3 shape. Then place the E4 shapes along the comb on each side of the rose and buds. When dry, glaze with water-based varnish.

These combs make beautiful, inexpensive gifts, especially when presented in a cellophane bag tied with ribbon.

Tortoise Shell Headband

Purchase one headband
Make one rose
Make two double buds
Make two single buds
Cut six E4 shapes
Cut six E3 shapes
Cut ten E6 shapes

With a cutting knife blade, etch the area of the headband where you will glue the dough to enable it to adhere easily. Roll out a sausage of green dough about 80 mm (3″) long and glue onto the etched area of the headband with a glue such as Aquadhere. When the base is dry (at least a day), place the rose in the centre with a double bud on each side. Place the single buds at each end together with two E3 shapes. Arrange the four remaining E3 shapes, two on each side, between the rose and the double buds. Glue one or two 10 mm (⅜″) stamens in the centre of each E3 shape, then place the E4 shapes along each side of the rose and buds. When dry, glaze with water-based varnish.

These headbands are great for children, or even a wedding headdress.

Children's Collection

Bunny, Heart, Butterfly, Teddy Bear and Bird Brooches

Purchase cutters in these shapes from toy shops or craft shops
For each brooch:
Make one single bud
Make one small rose
Cut one number 6 shape
Cut two E4 shapes

Cut out your chosen brooch base, smooth any rough edges with your fingers and leave to dry. Use the same flowers on each brooch base. Place a rose in the centre of each base with the bud beside it. Push shape number 6 into the side of the rose and bud with the handle end of a stitch unpicker. Place the E4 shapes either side of the rose and bud. Glue three 10 mm (⅜") stamens into the centre of the number 6 shape. Dry the brooch on a screen, glue on a brooch back, and glaze the brooch with water-based varnish.

These brooches are very popular with children.

Wreath of Flowers

24 cm (9½") length of fine craft wire
25 cm (9¾") length of bias binding
Make seven small roses
Cut seven number 6 shapes
Cut seven E1 shapes
Cut seven E4 shapes
Cut fourteen E2 shapes

Join the ends of the wire together to make a circle, then cover the wire with bias binding to give a good surface on which to glue the flowers. Glue the E2 shapes around the circle, placing each on an angle, and alternating so that one points in and the next points out and so on. Distribute the roses and other shapes evenly around the circle, pushing them gently into each other. Add one 10 mm (⅜") stamen to the number 6 shapes, and ball centres to the other shapes. When dry, glaze the wreath with water-based varnish.

You can make these wreaths big enough to fit a large hat, make a headpiece for a bride, or a necklace for that special low-cut dress.

Flower Cart Name Plaque

Purchase a wooden plaque
Cut a cardboard template 60 mm x 23 mm (2½" x 1")
Cut a cardboard template 70 mm x 20 mm (2¾" x ¾")
Use above templates to cut out one mould of white dough from each
template, for the cart
Make two roses
Make one single bud
Make three double buds
Cut two number 1 shapes
Cut three number 4 shapes
Cut two number 5 shapes
Cut two number 3 shapes

Cut five E4 shapes
Cut seven E2 shapes
Cut twelve E6 shapes

Sand the wood and paint it with your chosen colour. To make the flower cart, shape the sides of both pieces of dough you have cut out from the templates, so that the sides are angled in at the top and bottom of the cart as seen in the drawing.

Cut a small piece of dough in a sausage shape 15 mm (¾") long for the handle, and make two sausage shape lengths of dough 65 mm (2½") for the wheels. Cut ten 12 mm (½") sausage lengths for wheel spokes. Using a glue such as Aquadhere, arrange these pieces of dough on the plaque to resemble the cart in the drawing. Build up each end of the cart with the roses, then arrange number 1, number 4 and number 5 shapes so that they taper off to the centre of the cart. Add three 10 mm (⅜") stamens to the centre of the number 5 shapes. Push the E2 leaf shapes into the sides of the flowers all over the cart. Distribute the other shapes over the cart by using glue and gently pushing them into each other. Allow to dry for at least five days, then glaze the plaque with water-based varnish.

Train Name Plaque

Purchase a wooden plaque
Cut a cardboard template 45 mm x 25 mm (1½" x 1¼")
Cut five E3 shapes
Cut eight E4 shapes

Sand the wood and paint with your chosen colour. Write the person's name on the plaque in pencil, then paint over it. Roll out some white dough to about 5 mm (¼") thick and cut out three rectangles using the template. Cut three log shapes each 45 mm (1½") long. Cut a rectangle 20 mm x 17 mm (¾" x ⅝") for the cabin. Make two small round balls for the lights and a shape as in the drawing for the smoke funnel. Cut six wheels with the number 2 cutter. Using Aquadhere or similar, glue each piece onto the wooden plaque using the drawing as a guide. While the dough is

41

still wet, you can use a spatula to indent a pattern on parts of the train such as the windows and cabin doors. Using the handle end of a stitch unpicker, push gently into the middle of each wheel to give a realistic effect. When the train is dry, mix some paint (any colour you like) with water, and wipe it over the train with a sponge, letting it fill the indentations. Take a clean cloth and quickly remove the paint, leaving only the indentations coloured. Glue the five E3 and eight E4 shapes at the bottom and sides of the train. When the dough has dried, glaze the whole plaque with water-based varnish.

Hair Ribbon Holder

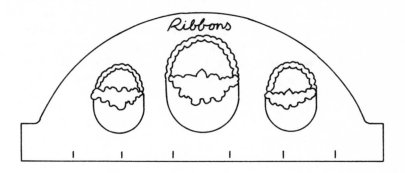

Purchase a wooden plaque
Six small brass hooks
Ball of white dough 5 cm (2") in diameter
Make four roses
Cut three number 5 shapes
Cut four number 4 shapes
Cut five number 1 shapes
Cut nine E1 shapes
Cut thirteen E2 shapes
Cut six E3 shapes
Cut six E4 shapes

Sand the wooden plaque and paint it in your chosen colour.
Write the word 'Ribbons' in pencil, then paint over it in
any colour you wish. Using scissors, cut from the dough
one large basket 75 mm wide by 55 mm deep (3" x 2¹/₅")
with a curved bottom and two smaller ones 55 mm wide
by 45 mm deep (2¹/₅ x 1⁴/₅") with curved bottoms. To make
handles, cut two sausage lengths for each basket, 100 mm
(4") in length for the large basket and 65 mm (2³/₅") in length
for the smaller baskets, and twist the two lengths together.

Glue the basket bases and handles onto the plaque as in the drawing. Make indents into the dough with a knife to give a plaited basket look. Using a glue such as Aquadhere arrange the same amount of flowers in each basket, putting any extra E1 and E2 shapes in the middle basket. Add two 10 mm (⅜") stamens to the centre of each number 5 shape, and ball centres to the other flower shapes. Cut extra flower shapes if you have gaps that need filling. When the dough has dried, mark the location of the brass hooks on the base of the plaque in pencil and screw them in. Glaze the entire plaque with water-based varnish.

right

left

45

Wood Collection
Decorative Door Wedge

Purchase a wooden door wedge
Make one large rose
Make two double buds
Make two single buds
Cut two number 5 shapes
Cut two number 4 shapes
Cut two number 1 shapes
Cut five E1 shapes
Cut six E2 shapes
Cut four E3 shapes

Sand the wood and paint it any colour you choose. Use Aquadhere or similar to glue pieces in position. Place the rose in the centre of the knob end of the wedge. Place the double buds on a slight angle and the single buds at the opposite angle around the rose. Place the E2 leaves at the ends of the buds and on each side of the rose. Add the number 5, 4 and 1 shapes to each side of the rose and buds, gently pushing them with the handle end of a stitch unpicker. At each end of the single buds, place two E1 and two E3 shapes. Add two stamens about 10 mm (⅜") long to the centre of each of the number 5 shapes. Glue tiny balls of dough into the centres of the remaining shapes. Allow at least four days to dry, then glaze the entire piece with water-based varnish.

Decorative Door Hanger

Purchase a wooden door hanger
Make three roses
Make two double buds
Make one single bud
Cut two number 4 shapes
Cut two number 5 shapes
Cut five E2 shapes
Cut four E3 shapes
Cut three E1 shapes
Cut three number 1 shapes

Sand the wood and paint any colour you prefer. Cream is a good colour as it complements the bread dough. Use Aquadhere or similar to glue pieces in position. Place the roses in the centre of the holder and arrange the E2 shapes around them. With the handle end of a stitch unpicker, gently mould the number 4 shapes and push them into the rose sides at each end. Fill the gaps with the remaining shapes. Add three stamens about 10 mm (⅜″) long to the centre of each of the number 5 shapes and a tiny ball of dough to all the remaining shapes. Allow at least four days to dry, then glaze the entire piece with water-based varnish.

Tissue Box Holder

Purchase a tissue box holder
Make two large roses
Make four double buds
Make four single buds
Cut two number 1 shapes
Cut four number 4 shapes
Cut four number 5 shapes
Cut eight E1 shapes
Cut twelve E2 shapes
Cut four E3 shapes

Sand the wood and paint inside and out in the colour of your choice. About 25 mm (1") from the opening on each side place one rose. Each side of the rose, place the double and single buds next to each other and arrange the E2 shapes as in the drawing. Arrange the number 4 and 5 shapes to each side of the roses and the number 1 shapes as in the drawing. Fill in the gaps on both sides evenly with the remaining shapes. Add two 10 mm (⅜") stamens to the centre of the number 5 shapes, and tiny balls of dough to the centre of all the other shapes. After about four days, when the dough is dry, glaze the entire box with water-based varnish.

This is a favourite of many of my clients. The tissue box may be varied simply by following the same procedure but altering the shapes used.

Napkin Holder

Purchase a wooden napkin holder
Make one rose
Make two double buds
Make two single buds
Cut two number 7 shapes
Cut two number 4 shapes
Cut two number 1 shapes
Cut six E2 shapes
Cut four E1 shapes

Sand the wood and paint it in your chosen colour. To prevent the napkin holder rolling while you work, anchor it with two sausage shapes of dough about 25 mm (1") long laid across the holder about 15 mm (½") apart. Press them down and allow to dry.

Place the rose in the middle of the holder, and arrange the double buds on a slight angle each side of the roses and place the single buds at the opposite angle. Glue two E2 shapes at each end of the buds, and the other four each side of the rose. Arrange the number 7, 4 and 3 shapes between the buds and the rose. Add two 10 mm (⅜") stamens to the centre of each number 7 shape. Fill the gaps with E1 shapes. When dry, glaze the entire holder with water-based varnish.

Photo Frame

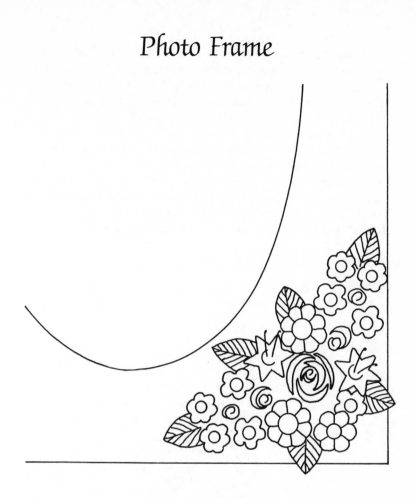

Purchase a wooden photo frame
Make two large roses
Make four double buds
Make four single buds
Cut four number 5 shapes
Cut four number 4 shapes
Cut two number 1 shapes
Cut eight E4 shapes
Cut ten E1 shapes
Cut twelve E2 shapes

53

Sand the wood and paint in the colour of your choice. Glue pieces in position with Aquadhere or similar. When the paint is dry, place one rose in the top left-hand corner and the other in the bottom right-hand corner. Place a double and single bud either side of each rose and six E2 shapes around each group of roses and buds, as in the drawing. Place two number 5, 4 and one number 1 shapes at each corner around the rose and buds. Distribute the E1 and E4 shapes evenly between the two corners. Glue two 10 mm (⅜") stamens into the centre of each number 5 shape, and tiny balls of dough in the centre of the other shapes. Allow to dry and then glaze the entire frame with water-based varnish.

Decorative Hand Mirror

Purchase a wooden framed mirror
Make three roses
Make two double buds
Make one single bud
Cut two number 5 shapes
Cut one number 4 shape
Cut one number 1 shape
Cut one number 3 shape
Cut one number 6 shape
Cut six E1 shapes
Cut seven E2 shapes

Remove the mirror before sanding and painting the wood. When the paint is dry, position mirror back in place then position the three roses at the top of the handle with a double bud at each side. Place one single bud above the mirror. Place five E2 shapes around the roses and two above the mirror as in the drawing. Place the number 6 and 3 shapes and one E1 shape above the mirror. Gently push the number 1, 5 and 4 shapes into the sides of the roses. Fill the gaps with the remaining E1 shapes. Cut four 10 mm (⅜") long stamens and glue two stamens into the centre of each number 5 shape. Glue tiny balls of dough in the centre of the other shapes. After about four days, when the dough is dry, glaze the entire piece with water-based varnish.

Candle Holder

Purchase a wooden candle holder
Make three large roses
Make six double buds
Cut six number 5 shapes
Cut three number 4 shapes
Cut six number 6 shapes
Cut three E1 shapes
Cut nine E2 shapes
Cut six E4 shapes

Sand and paint the wood in the colour of your choice. Space the roses equally around the rim of the holder. Place the double buds each side of the roses, and the E2 shapes around the roses and buds. Position the number 5, 4 and 6 shapes evenly around the roses and buds. Fill the gaps with the E1 and E4 shapes. Place two 10 mm (⅜") stamens in each number 5 shape, and a tiny ball of dough in the centre of the other flower shapes. After about four days, when the dough has dried, glaze the entire holder with water-based varnish.

You can use any shape of candle holder — just rearrange the flowers to suit the shape.

Jewellery Box

Make three roses
Make two double buds
Make one single bud
Make three number 4 shapes
Make three number 5 shapes
Make five number 8 shapes
Make six E1 shapes

Sand the wood and paint in your chosen colour. Use Aquadhere or similar to glue pieces in place. Place roses in the centre of the top of the box and glue the number 8 shapes in a circle approximately 12 mm (½") out from the roses. Place double and single buds around roses. Place the number 4 shapes in between the roses, then add the number 5 shapes next to the number 4 shapes. Fill in the gaps with the E1 shapes and glue two 10 mm (⅜") stamens into the number 5 shapes. When dry, glaze the entire box with water-based varnish.

Wooden Cottage Thimble

Purchase a wooden thimble
Prepare a quantity each of green, brown,
white and yellow dough

Sand the thimble and paint it in your chosen colour. Make a ball of dark green dough and using Aquadhere or similar, glue it on the top of the thimble, squeezing it down over the edges so that it resembles a hill. With a larger ball of white dough, make a brick shape and glue it on top of the hill a little off centre. Make the roof with a rectangle of brown dough moulded over the top of the white shape, and indent the roof with a darning needle to make it resemble corrugated iron. Glue a small piece of brown dough to the side of the cottage for the tree trunk, and a ball of green dough on top of the trunk. Pick at the green ball with a pin to make it resemble the foliage of a tree. Make the garden path with a little yellow dough and pattern it with a small knife. Glue three tiny balls of green dough to each side of the path and pick at them with a pin to make them resemble tiny bushes. When the dough is completely dry, paint in the door and windows in the front and back of the cottage. When dry, glaze the whole thimble with water-based varnish.

This cottage thimble is one of my favourite designs.

Flower Thimble

Purchase a wooden thimble
Make one rose
Make one number 4 shape
Make one number 5 shape
Make one E1 shape
Make one E3 shape

Sand the thimble and paint with your chosen colour. Use Aquadhere or similar to glue shapes in position. Position the rose off centre on top of the thimble. Place the number 4 and 5 shapes on either side of the rose. In between the rose and number 4 shape, place the E1 shape, and in between the rose and the number 5 shape, place the E3 shape. Place two 10 mm (⅜″) stamens into the centre of the number 5 shape. Using the ball end of a berri pin glue balls of coloured dough into the centre of the remaining shapes. When dry, glaze entire thimble with water-based varnish.

Other Books in the Milner Craft Series